An Algebra

DON BOGEN

An Algebra

THE UNIVERSITY OF CHICAGO PRESS

Chicago & London

DON BOGEN is professor of English at the University of Cincinnati. He is the author of a critical study of Theodore Roethke and three previous books of poetry: *After the Splendid Display*, *The Known World*, and *Luster*.

The University of Chicago Press, Chicago 60637
The University of Chicago Press, Ltd., London
© 2009 by The University of Chicago
All rights reserved. Published 2009
Printed in the United States of America
18 17 16 15 14 13 12 11 10 09   1 2 3 4 5

ISBN-13: 978-0-226-06313-3 (paper)
ISBN-10: 0-226-06313-5 (paper)

Library of Congress Cataloging-in-Publication Data
Bogen, Don.
    An algebra / Don Bogen.
        p. cm. — (Phoenix poets series)
    ISBN-13: 978-0-226-06313-3 (pbk. : alk. paper)
    ISBN-10: 0-226-06313-5 (pbk. : alk. paper)
    I. Title. II. Series: Phoenix poets.
    PS3552.O4337A79 2009
    811'.54—dc22   2008039233

For my parents

CONTENTS

ACKNOWLEDGMENTS

Grateful acknowledgment is made to the following journals in which some of the poems in this book first appeared, sometimes in different versions:

Colorado Review: "Air," "Sky," and "Who"
Electronic Poetry Review: "Barcarole," "Edge," "Have To," and "Slash"
FIELD: "Vaporizer"
The New Republic: "Flowers" and "Run"
Partisan Review: "Could Not Speak" and "Give It Back"
Ploughshares: "Bagatelles" and "Proteus"
Poetry: "Variations on an Elegiac Theme"
The Southeast Review: "An Algebra"
Sou'Wester: "A World"

Sections of this book were set to music by Allen Otte and performed by him in "As an Algebra," recorded on the CD *Implements of Actuation*. "Variations on an Elegiac Theme," under the title "1886," received the 1997 *The Writer* / Emily Dickinson Award from the Poetry Society of America.

I am grateful to the Camargo Foundation, the University of Cincinnati Charles Phelps Taft Research Center, the Corporation of Yaddo, the Ohio Arts Council, and the National Endowment for the Arts for grants that allowed me to complete this book.

I

RUN

Wanted solitude, feared it
Wanted to run, always somewhere new
Blank streets of the poor blocks, front yards with chain-link fence
Hospital buildings sealed, monumental
Wanted no faces in the windows, no visitors coming with roses

At places to turn back kept going
Wanted the loop larger, taking more in
Small abandoned factories that made boxes, candy, soap
Soot-fuzzed louvers, glass underfoot
Wanted the lungs to tighten—three, then two steps to a breath

Wanted solitude, kept turning off the big streets
Found loose dogs growling in driveways, car parts on porches
Sidewalks swallowed in weeds
Gravel—wanted the slide of gravel at sudden dead ends
Having to turn back uphill

Wanted to slow but would not stop
Wanted to come back some different way
Yellow lamp glow of other lives
Old parking lots, the closed-off stories of cars
Dreamed up over and over

Wanted nothing known, all to be imagined
Glint of winter sunlight off windows
Late streets empty, echoes muffled on brick
Feared solitude but wanted the loop larger
Wanted everything breath could hold

Proteus

To take,
         like water,
whatever shape you flow through, fill, or rest in.

And to choose that shape.

         *   *   *

As: Brian, become a gangster,
six feet from my face.
Voice no longer a caress
but a sharpened projection,
belly a ram in a buttoned vest.

The whole body shows
                        the thing done:
goat-song in the rites of a god,
transforming, starting to speak now
through him
              as he walks on stage.

         *   *   *

Remember when you turned
into moonlight, the bark of an oak,
an orange going to shreds
in your own cold palm?

Everything you saw
                you *were*,
and you saw everything.

No choice.
That face light gnarled around a tree
was your face.

        * * *

Flesh is approximate.
We clothe it in dreams,
wrestling with our eyes closed
down through layers:
                        thug, wraith,
chieftain, devouring angel (held
by my shoulders I
am trying to make you
stay put) daddy mama breath
balm a man a woman in
separate desires
                overlapped.

        * * *

Curious,
        cautious enough
to disguise himself as a woman,
the voyeur peeks at the rite.

Women, leaping, mothers and daughters—
their rapt beauty draws him out.

The god
      has tricked him:
they will tear him apart.

     * * *

As: a virus.
      Never alive,
but a frantic mimicry of life
to pierce the cell, make over
its orders, move, repeat itself, mutate
in sped-up mini-evolution—
now it swims the blood, unravels
in light, never alive, now
                it floats on air.

Lost in the host a thousand years,
inert chemical mechanism
asleep in a rain-forest cave.

     * * *

To mime—
      not a statue
or a gray accountant picked from the crowd,
but a robot.

Steel jumpsuit and boots,
greasepaint turning the eyelids
aluminum.

This hand a crank, this grin
the edge of a disk,
                    I am Mister
Silver Mister Silver—tape
loop syncopating
over the drum machine.

     *   *   *

As: a child's toy,
its intricate language of joints and swivels,
creature within creature:
the robot
                    a wolf on silver feet,
in his boxy jaw
the tiny half-robotic
head of a man
                    who will drive the car.

     *   *   *

Who will drive the car
                    to the hospital
after the cancer has metastasized?

     *   *   *

These knots rising in my palm—
look, in the photo album,
he grips the mower like a sad hawk.

Grandfather, father, son—flesh
tightens, branching genes
send up more
                    of the claw each year.

After the operation
skin comes back thick as bark.

      * * *

A boy, a lion, wild boar,
snake no one will touch
holds the changes.

Dream he is a sea god,
                    and he is.
Dream he is a stone, a bull, no,
a tree
        rippling over
the waves' quick light, he is
shape always becoming, he is a flame
and the stream that drowns it.

A Cage

Tunnels through black earth, through
bone:
       goldfish fat as biscuits
probe the bulged veins,
chambers of cartilage,
in one a scarred pike
flipped
       in a knot.

Dreams in this grotto
of foreign dark—I can't
unpack them.

Betrayal? Guilt?
This was about something I'd
forgotten.

     * * *

Intricate, web-sticky
texture of regret:
           the past
a net of roots finding
no hold,
      the present endless
writhing in the net.

Wrestling, blind
wrestling—the nest
sinks
        into itself,
sticks, brown leaves, dry stems
enumerate old themes.

     * * *

Why does the lake still
rim my dreams?

Beach, small breakers, sandbars—
layers of horizon
                the moon keeps remaking,
a border through years of sleep.

Always a comfort, that blue-gray lip
under cloud fields. It
blocks off the east,
                    seals what's passed.
The edge is something you can't see across.

     * * *

Dusk on a boulevard,
wet snow thickening nostalgia.
That bottle-green light from a showroom,
blurred, enticing,
                in all the objects
lined up on the walls.

Car parts? Or plates?
Or door chimes?
                    Row on row—
drive on, there's nothing anyone could want.

     *   *   *

I am in this tunnel
in a car, driving back from some talk,
pneumonia still wrestling my lungs.

Memory has garnered,
                    embellished
the swoops and stacked interchanges,
neon in the gleaming tubes
extending and bending
                    cool orange light—

but not the talk, grit in my cough,
whatever mall we stopped at.

     *   *   *

Each cold
another step to deafness.

Fog gathers
around the fast delicate consonants
of talk in a crowd, a whispered joke,
the single cricket
                    I watched making sound.

Invisible distance
year on year deepening,
slow retreat—

a ghost pretends to be alive.

    *   *   *

A frame makes a window
you can't see out.

Bars, locks,
steel-colored button shapes to press,
and the comforting illusions:
time a quaint archaic hourglass,
motion a scroll at your control.

Enter:
        your life infinite layers
where everything is flat.
Point, shrink, and close till the screen goes blank.

    *   *   *

Old people falling,
people forgetting,
                forgetting
they fell.

This skeletal box—
aluminum tubes like the bed rails,

black rubber caps on its rocking
legs—
             a walker
that helps you walk
toward the door, your
helpless son and daughter,
                              toward
a memory of them.

        *   *   *

Found himself kindly,
a companionable ghost
at the party's edge
nursing—
             rage? despair?—
absurdly in a plastic cup.

Time went on blanching him:
a voice, thinning,
                    that might sparkle
amid the chorus a moment,
another voice fixed
in the empty cage of ink.

Get this down now
                    so it will last,
drink this and disappear.

WANTS

There's nothing anyone could want
A yard sale where the private past is suddenly on display
Brought up from storage, dazed and blinking
Drugstore lamps, dessert glasses, AM clock radio
The two-speed bicycle you stripped down over the years
Worth more if it still had its tank, fins, and handlebar streamers
What moves and what doesn't—you can't sell it all
On card tables old desires transpose into *objets d'art* and junk
The basement empties like the hold of a freighter
So you can get away

AIR

Air as lost time
Voice of a cloud, of a ghost crowned with nimbus
Smack-thin, it lingers forty years
I thought it came from the jeweled world we'd seen
Everything stuffed, urgent, glittering alive
But it was just pleasure, blank and sure
Now what is there to sing
From speakers, the tune folds and fades in waves
Earphones drive it through your head

WHO

Broken—who goes there
A Christmas innocence watery with nostalgia
Burnt herb smell blurring the years
War has its long fingers, love its old haunts
That ice-cream shop, her paisley skirt
The purple commas swirling as if animated by sight
Full-body armor of a tingling cloud
Encased, I pictured tracer rounds as a light show
Sweet smoke, what are you singing
The boy almost a man who'd be a child

EDGE

The edge is something you can't see across
Burnt-out refineries on the rim of a winter city
Trainyards, coal piles, empty pre-fab warehouses
No people but a clutter of abandonment
Against a straight blank sky
Fixed now, pointed toward abstraction, the scene waits
You stare at what you've made and keep seeing more
White space mirrors a mind of ice
Snow only suggests the distances and threats

HAVE TO

What do you have to give away
One note—you break it open again and again
A braid of tones inside the one tone unraveling
As it drowns in air like all tones
Same mind, same wrist, same hand, same white key like a chisel
Repeated, a moment thickens
Focus clears out what's messy and unimportant
The deeper you listen the more you hear the limits
There is no world this infinite and pure

SWIM

They are swimming in the book
Two stick pens on the yellow pad where I left them
The random now suddenly purpose, configuration
An almost-V catching a moment's light
Glint as of crystal off the faceted surfaces
Inside, veins with drying traces
Streaks in a wineglass, residue of streams
Under the long-visored caps a black reservoir, a blue
Go with me little pools

Vaporizer

A charm,
        a dream of protection.
Gurgles hold the night light's glow.

A stream of clouds
               misting the branching tubes.

Water, in fog, a tub, plug to
wire in the wall saying

Okay, it's okay all night.

      *   *   *

School, a door closing
he opens:
         haze of playground French,
the five names for different kinds of marbles,
games, bullies he wandered among
while I was staring at the sea.

Shut off,
not my past,
           nothing I could do—

I keep making up
all the world he lived.

His new name, intricate drawings of aliens,
long tunnel of lunch
(*Mais il ne mange rien monsieur*)—
school hours shadows

                that smother my days.

      *   *   *

Burnt-out hills:
char and velvety ash

                along the dropped limbs,
magpies, new gullies.

A dry time clears the ground.

He was standing where the road split,
arms spread, a small *x*
straddling the crack.
That bird call a slash, then,
on the edge of things.

He was standing,

             behind him
the green blue of ocean, the white blue of sky.

      *   *   *

The house of childhood sold,
or razed—

not lost but

         softened, distended:
diaphanous linked chambers springing from

a lightshaft or a varnish smell,
the way a floorboard aches,
a scrap of wallpaper

                tunnels the heart.

       * * *

A film of
        "events"—
tiny collisions, tracks of light
in the bubble chamber—you'd scan
for hours (smell of formica, rock headsets,
eyes going furry near four AM).

This celluloid memory now
your memory, coursing
chemical fissures in the brain.

Matter split like time,
                  thinner and thinner parings—
Anything that happens is too fast to see

       * * *

There the sky kept reeling as she ran—
wisps, then puffy clumps,
then rain—
         the park spread low
beneath the blanketing.

Who could have worn
that purple coat
cartwheeling in the grass?

It grows
        as I look at it,
puts on pillowy layers.

Now the coat wears memory,
warms a ghost.

        *   *   *

Wind off the world's top,
whipped clouds over hedgerows:
Girton, that one year
twenty years away.

He learned to walk, she started school,
read, slowly,
            the first book *Red*.

Moss edging the garden wall,
little flags on the clothesline.

A Language

Thirty years swept open—
milkweed
　　　　　transfigures the field.

How she changed him,
he her,
　　　　a bird cry
defining the territory.

Possession, of the past,
of place—those hills,
that coast—
　　　　　of the nest:

she marks him,
he her,
　　　　seizing distances.

　　　*　*　*

This music of scenes
we shuttle between us,
ever more interwoven
as measures blur over time:

a walk,
yes, I, then
                a meal, rush
and slow of ocean through
drawn shades
somewhere when—
                notes
held, grouped, changed, repeated,
overflowing the score.

     * * *

Loops and swirls I know
from messages on the phone table—
page after page of them
now your hand is ink.

The story grows:
facts, dates, events—
                I don't
need the news but
a sigh
        breathing hieroglyphs,
my fingertips reading
the scroll of your back.

Voice
        in the mind,
I want your wet mouth,
not this paper
that rattles in the wind.

     * * *

Eyes too
      undress—
that pale look they take on
with your glasses off.

A thin blue
fragile, almost violet
in the moon shell,
pink
     lip at the rim,
softened pupil that can't read
my too-close face.

Study me now,
focus the dark.
        Eyes,
when my tongue speaks you are slits.

     *   *   *

A call of flesh,
a lesson learned
to re-learn—
      What
are you saying each
moment I need
to hear again—
        our hands
listen, mouths
pushed open as the point drives home.

     *   *   *

Your hair
shades of wheat at first,
of oak,
             now more soft ash
each night we burn.
My forest, my playground, my nest.

Delirious waterfall—years
swirl in my hands,
moonlight flooding
                        a darkened room.

            *   *   *

Metaphors: she
                    is damp earth
and I the plow, drawn
to the source of this old noun
husband.

No, to sighs,
mere sounds—
                    no,
not sounds merely but
a language of shifting
touch where she is
limb bud fruit trunk blossom

FLOWERS

And brought home flowers then
The glad blue iris, bright carnation
Bouncing on top of the laundry basket
In a white car on thin roads
Passing hedges and plowed fields in the rain

And brought them flowers
The wife pleased, arranging
The schoolgirl's glee when she came home
The baby reaching up toward them
As he would toward the rising of the sun

East wind over the moss wall and garden
Sky and shadow streaming by the window
In the gray row house, two up two down
The little square of family then
A frame around the table at dusk

And brought home this gesture with the clean wash
A curve of color marking Wednesdays
Each week the fish man, vegetable man
A new word in the schoolgirl's books
The baby's eyes and hands

And drove home each week through stone villages
Girton, Histon, the names blurring
Smoke from allotment gardens on the wind then
Berries in wet hedgerows
Red as any blood

II

VARIATIONS ON AN ELEGIAC THEME

A stillness in
the air you heard
a fly buzz in as

between them and silence
the blanket that would
hold you blank as air

that circles the dear
globe turning erasing
in heaves of storm

Your stillness resting
in the calm between
measures a current

under the layers strands
of bound air that
gather to wrest

voice from an empty
rush to resist
in dashed song

A stillness interset
with breath clouds
on the world's shell

of gas parentheses
between us and the dark
effacing waves your brief

lines altering the fall
of light you could
see to see

Bagatelles

What ghost threw
                  my hand across my face?
He roamed my sleep
in that room dark under pines.

Another cried softly for an hour,
till comforted.

Lakes, mansion, woods, studios—
all of it loss
               and the love of art.

Mornings I'd stare at an old story:
the touring car draped in a tarp,
wet grass, a little lump
where all the children lay.

    * * *

Skin as stone.
Strokes of green and ocher defining
a thin light.
What the eye sees,
the hand, he knew,
               can make.

Perfection, that sphinx calm,
eludes and terrifies.
He sang to it.

Solitude, he demanded perfect solitude,
stared into himself,

                    came to love death.

     *   *   *

When she came back from Bali,
what she heard most clearly
was silence:

               smooth, continuous,
framed merely
by the hushed tide of traffic.

Music deliberate,

                 set apart:
no talking in the festivals,
no wind chimes marking
air as lost time.

     *   *   *

Lip to lip,
breath moving over the silver mouth—
the air turns new shapes
as you work with it,

                following changes.

A long open sigh, a slit,
each tone has its own needs
and calls to make you—
                                    where,
now, where?—
                    nip and sway,
rising to meet it.

     *   *   *

Flesh music had caught up once
sinks and aches.

She slumps in khaki,
slow fear edging her eyes.

A dancer's instrument
sags in its time—
                    so the art *is* loss,
a curse its precise, relentless
beat: What do you have,
what do you have to give away?

     *   *   *

Three pen nibs over the rim of a box,
pencil tips sharpened for different uses,
brush, corked jar of blue ink set
carefully
            on the sketchbook.

That study of his tools
a prayer to potential, a blessing
on gifts:
            his room,
an hour of sea breeze through a window,
working in watercolors the light fades.

            *   *   *

Bagatelles,
mere gestures
                in dry air,
each pluck a dot,
strokes marked on silence
reaching into the dark.

Beauty is strict,
                it passes:

an echo, a wedge
of harmony, sudden,
broken—*Who goes there?*

Barcarole

These waves
            pushing *out* to sea,
whitecaps erupting where wind
shoves against the pulse.

Tilt of the globe,
                    pull of the moon
day and night, this roar
down a river valley—
all fighting in the bay.

Froth not curtains but veils
skittering over wavetops,
                    a surface
turquoise at first light, wrinkled slate at dusk.

    * * *

Noon slapped the graveyard.
Sun-wracked poppies in clay pots,
a steep, dessicated rest.

Strict clock,
            lopped calendar:
time in gravel dust, drawers of ash
climbing the hill behind me.

    * * *

Where is she?

In the lines
of another student, in hers,
in memory,
            in the earth.

The words change,
they are swimming in the book.

            *   *   *

These leaves—
which are, he said,
grass.

Ubiquitous, democratic
hair on the graves
                of young men.

Not a book but
a tonic to filter the blood—
                    read them,
read them in the open air every day of your life.

            *   *   *

Research:
his brain a blood sponge,
a daybook, open, in the operating theater
(dead so it doesn't matter),
the friend sifting microscope slides
as if they were his ashes.

What message,
        where?

The skull coffer's
empty. No spot in the brain
for Göttingen,
        for love.

Pages turn, memory-thin—
nothing more to read.

    * * *

Who will drive the car
               to the hospital
after the cancer has metastasized?

    * * *

A sketch of roofs
in Mediterranean light,
rapid,
        tiles drying
from a winter shower,
kitchen gardens,
            vines
over fences caught
in the moment and
beneath it all the abstract
planes and angles
           drawing the eye
(deliberate, inevitable),

starting
        to reassert themselves
as the clouds clear.

      *　*　*

The sea as elegy:
slap and meter of its surface,
reminding, erasing,
and the slow changes below.

What holds
        erodes,
or diverges in filtered light:

coral growing skeletons,
picked bones, shells
sinking into stone.

SKY

The green blue of ocean, the white blue of sky
When he looks up from chopping brush, he is lost in the sun
Disease has glazed and freed him
His forgetting skims across creek beds and hills to the Pacific
A dry glint that dazzles, revealing nothing
It shears off the past, shears history
Can anyone survive such innocence
The heart is strong, body flexible
A smile and wave fixed in the reflexes

READ

Nothing more to read
History has its orders: conquistadors, then literate friars
At Uxmal pages blackened in the hot glow
Records of the moon and stars, rules for sacrifice
Not hieroglyphs but marks that became speech
Unintelligible, barbarian, shrieking in the flames like demons
Preserved now, the conquest lies sleeping in the padre's book
Writing recalls what will always be lost
Fire burns out that recollection

STAGE

As he walks on stage
The president of fruit spreads his name in legacy
His business school, his family amphitheater
A museum he paid for, with a hall of heroes
His name gleams on the monitor among others: Gandhi, César Chávez
Brilliant in pixels, it will always be remembered
The fruit company never existed now
History is a billboard to be painted over
The paint is money, the money blood

ANYTHING THAT HAPPENS

Anything that happens is too fast to see
But I watched it—there are pictures in the album
Less than a second's light fixed in chemicals
Little boxes under a vinyl sheet gone cloudy now
What are these dyes that fade at the surface
That child face you wear still under your skin
Whenever I look nothing changes
A photo gives the residue of a lost moment
It claws at memory like a drowning swimmer
Who will not be saved

SLASH

The myriad slash and burn
Where are my armies of die-cut cardboard
Map grids, battle charts, dice in the felt-lined cup
Gettysburg and Normandy worlds at thirteen I could half control
History was my door closed, playing both sides
Boxes that engulfed me crumble in the landfill
Soaked and rotting, the worms eating through
Each small thing I make now holds its edge
As if to cut off time

GIVE IT BACK

Give it back—I made it all up
That alcove where surplus glowed under dust
Unfinished, an attic space with nails poking down
Khaki of sheet metal, orange flickering in tubes
Ephemeral as the smells, which were plywood, solder, and Kents
Color words, smell words—I put them in a book
Everything there is still missing
Two lies of remembrance: it was always winter
Things could speak

A World

In the jam:
            stalled, clotting,
heatwaves from the hoods,
airport
            an impossible walk away.

A woman, caught in despair
at the stopped wheel,
soundless, behind glass,
as her life is made part of this.

        *   *   *

The American plan—no
breakfast, no free lunch,
just husks of great cities, withering.

The ripples pulse outward,
detritus at the core:
skeletal towers jagging a stubble field,
shell-crater parking lots,
                        your car
out on the windy avenues,
adrift among the middens,
the myriad slash and burn.

        *   *   *

A frame makes a window
you can't see out.

Bars, locks,
steel-colored button shapes to press,
and the comforting illusions:
time a quaint archaic hourglass,
motion a scroll at your control.

Enter:
          your life infinite layers
where everything is flat.
Point, shrink, and close till the screen goes blank.

          *   *   *

The silicon workshops of Seoul:
women gowned and masked,
magnifiers, soldering irons
thin as hypodermics.

How many channels are on your TV,
each one framing
                    the pulsations of changing light?
They leap from the wired decisions.

          *   *   *

Beach, alleys, port, market,
rich hills—
          all the city's sweet flesh,

her swells, dips, and soft turnings
littered with needles, littered with needles.

     * * *

War names:
            Cointelpro,
Brilliant Pebbles, Operation This,
then That, and That—

so many,
          I had not thought,

endless, blurred, compacted
like Gitmo,
          the newsmen
embedded in their tanks.

     * * *

There were guards
and a wall I shot under
on the U-Bahn.

I remember
rifles in dim tunnels,
damp abandoned platforms.
I remember
        Look at these
shoes this money what is it worth?

The train of memory
                    on a vacant spur,
the train of history shunted
to the shopping mall.

        *   *   *

The plane is a room
sliced out of time.

Party-in-a-box:
                    sad drinks, food, chatter
among the headsets and hectic laptops,
your book a box inside the box,
opened like a stopped watch.

Nobody moves
                    and the world slides away.

An Algebra

Two moons, refracted,
an hour before dawn.

The black-coffee edge of things
in heavy air.

I was
        hurrying, hurrying,
crossing in front of car lights, two
half-disks overlapped through the lenses,
the dream face splintered, mocking.

            *   *   *

Mask of a face,
                of my face:
skull box with the skin pulled over it,
a map of plains and crevices
jumbled in seismic disturbance
and the sag of erosion,
a history of insignificant skirmishes
on pocked vellum,
stage set
            and falling curtain,
the only newspaper
I read every day.

            *   *   *

Messages contrived
               and left
on paper, tape, or screen, waiting
in filings, in invisible
flicked switches.

The net widens,
its calls and cries
               diffuse,
ever fainter demands, knots
unraveling—
               I have been
negligent—
               in the end all
holes,
a veil of dust passing
through empty space.

       *   *   *

The house of childhood sold,
or razed—

not lost but
               softened, distended:
diaphanous linked chambers springing from
a lightshaft or a varnish smell,
the way a floorboard aches,
a scrap of wallpaper
               tunnels the heart.

       *   *   *

Cachot, oubliette—
a language turns over
its roots that,
hidden, forgotten,
                    still
outlive names scratched on a wall.

Who was here?
                    Words
whirling in the dictionary,
bodies in a keep, left.

            *   *   *

I can't remember
what I forgot
                    in the dream.

A deed or some contract
obliging, a last required class, lost
child, the house collapsing on its
untended foundations as I learn
before the sudden waking
once more,
                    I can't
remember

Give it back—I made it all up.

            *   *   *

The wing of the hospital
folds under itself

and drops.

Trucks in the rubble,
a crane
          dangling its jaws on cables.

Brick skin stripped away,
then plaster and the barer functions:
wires, airshafts,
a water line connecting each
private sink.

        *   *   *

There is a memory
                    I can't remember,
a closed room where I couldn't
speak.

Big foam earphones
of the fifties, tape reels
I know from photographs,

something about the sounds, I
couldn't say:
                    s's that lisped, waddling *r*'s,
stuttering—everything then, speech, this
music my tongue aches to taste
stopped, in my throat, caught, everything
a compensation?

        *   *   *

Landscape of walls in the afternoons:
stucco the color of warm milk,
ocher tiles and, higher,
shutters sealed in sleep.

The hills slip away from the town.

Dry gravel flap
              of my heart as I ran
past a house called *sans souci*,
a house called *carpe diem*.

    *   *   *

A camera teaches you light,
its texture—

not shafts of a god
through clouds, not a blank glow
or a pinprick laser, but
moments
              this low sun marks
passing over thyme, mimosa,
and scrub oak,
                            paths
your eyes caress, tracing
depth, the shadows' touch.

    *   *   *

An algebra,
its shifting equivalents:

numbers with their stated values,
and letters, italicized, interchangeable,
rippling in the balance pans.

The trick is
                    that nothing's lost.

A magical innocence.
This operation sets the bones
to reunite the broken parts.

COULD NOT SPEAK

Could not speak but only arrange
Made tiles in a tile factory, painted on them
Nine different scenes: trees on cliffs, vineyards, estates
Permanent, unreachable under the glaze
Could not speak but worked at a table with others
Signed the clients' names
Breathed clay, clay wash on my fingernails

In fall made crèche figures, painted them
Simplified folds of the swaddling
Two dots for eyes, lips one red stroke
God after God after God
Could not speak but arranged them in lines
Cut off the excess, smashed the defective
Mixed paint, fed the oven, baked and made them

Flat scenes, little men, little animals
In lines as if they were an army marching
Sold at the fair: cut off and wrapped up
Hung on walls or set out at holidays
Stiff, bone-light, caught in sheen
Could not speak but was everywhere
Maker of what is made